Embertides

Suite for Organ

HILARY TANN

*Commissioned by the American Guild of Organists
for the 2014 Biennial National Convention
in Boston, Mass.*

MUSIC DEPARTMENT

OXFORD
UNIVERSITY PRESS

OXFORD
UNIVERSITY PRESS

Great Clarendon Street, Oxford OX2 6DP,
United Kingdom

Oxford University Press is a department of the University of Oxford.
It furthers the University's aim of excellence in research, scholarship,
and education by publishing worldwide. Oxford is a registered trade mark
of Oxford University Press in the UK and in certain other countries

First published 2014

Impression: 1

ISBN 978-0-19-339901-3

Music origination by Jon Bunker

Printed in Great Britain on acid-free paper by
Caligraving Ltd, Thetford, Norfolk

Contents

Composer's note

Embertides consists of four separate movements that take their inspiriation from the roughly equal divisions of the church year—Advent, Lent, Whitsun, and Michaelmas. These divisions in turn pay homage to earlier, secular traditions—Winter (seeding), Spring (awakening), Summer (harvesting), and Autumn (vintage). The cycle is unified by references to verses from the 11th-century plainsong sequence 'Veni Sancte Spiritus'; in addition, each piece contains hints of hymns appropriate to each season. The work may be performed as a concert suite or individual movements may be used separately within church services.

The composer is grateful to Alfred V. Fedak (Albany, NY) for his professional assistance in selecting appropriate organ registrations.

Duration: 15 mins (Advent: 3'20", Lenten 3'40", Whit 3'40", Michaelmas 4'00")

Embertides was first performed by Heinrich Christensen at the National Convention of the American Guild of Organists, June 25 and 26, 2014, at the First Church in Boston, MA.

1. Advent (Winter)

HILARY TANN

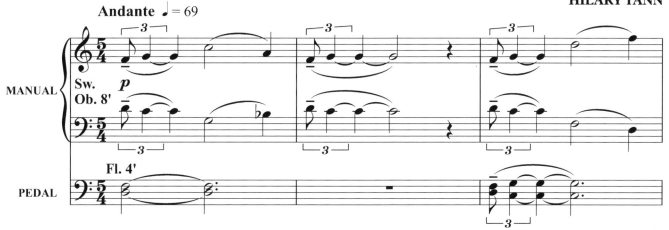

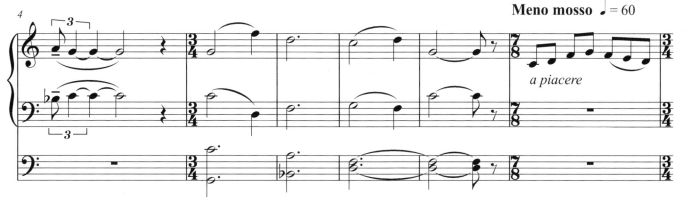

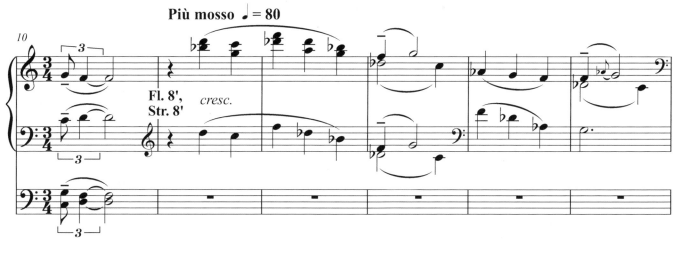

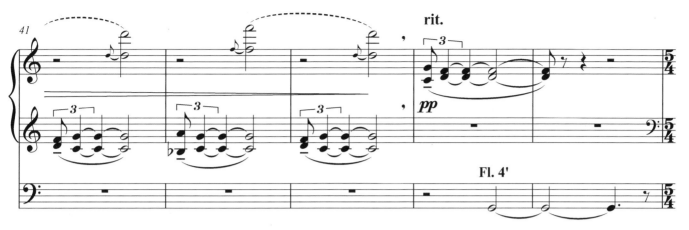

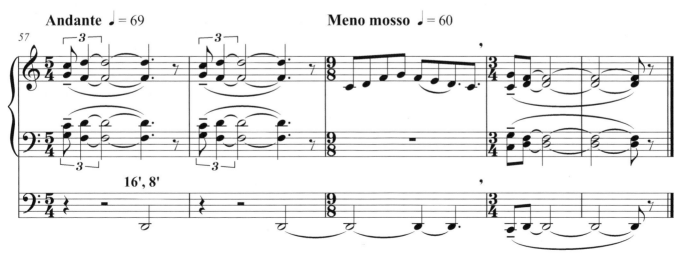

4

2. Lenten (Spring)

Sw.: Fl. 8', 2'
Ch.: 8', 2⅔'
Ped.: 16', 8'

HILARY TANN

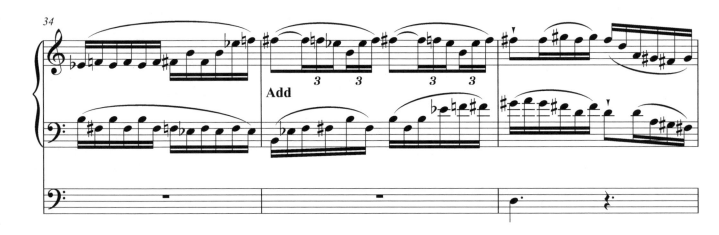

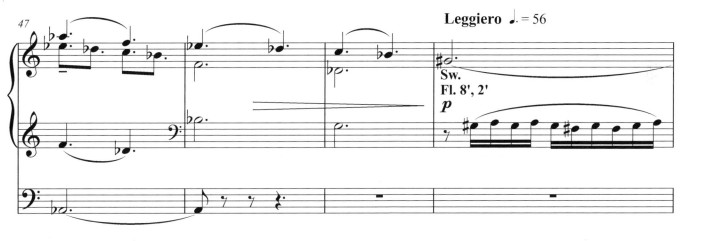

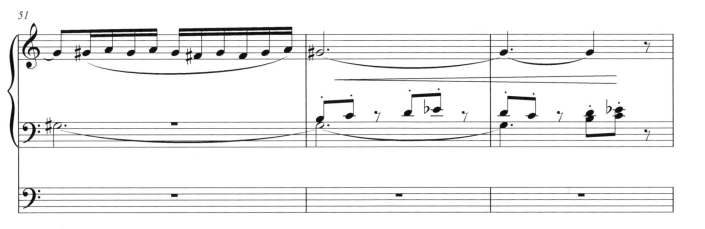

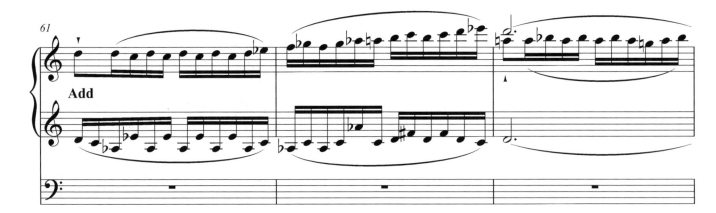

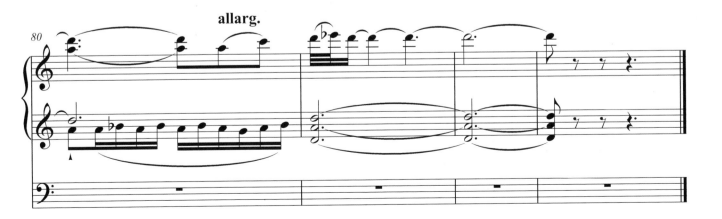

3. Whit (Summer)

Sw.: Fl. 8', 4', 8' str. cel., 4' couplers
Ped.: Fl. 4', Pr. 2'

HILARY TANN

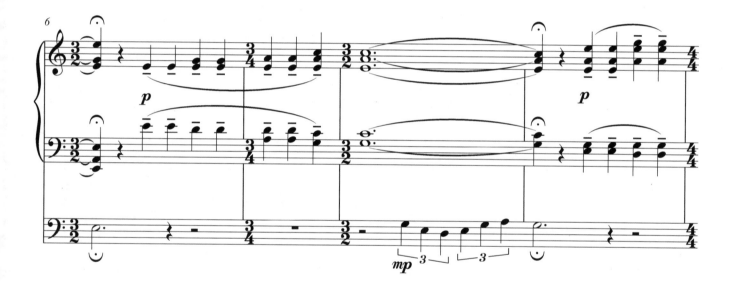

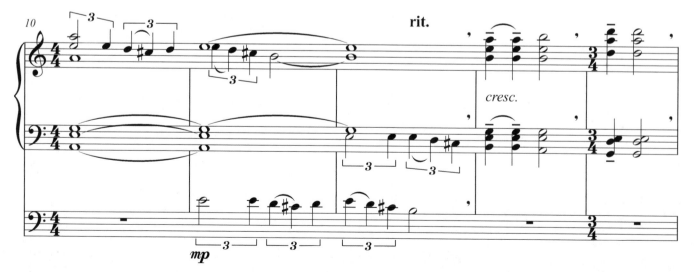

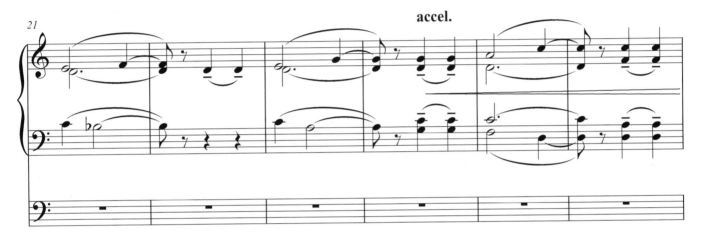

12

Più vivo ♩ = 80

16', 8'

rit. al fine

4. Michaelmas (Autumn)

Gt.: Pr. 8', Fl. 4'
Sw.: Pr. 8', 4', mixture
Ped.: 16', 8'

HILARY TANN

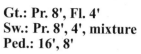

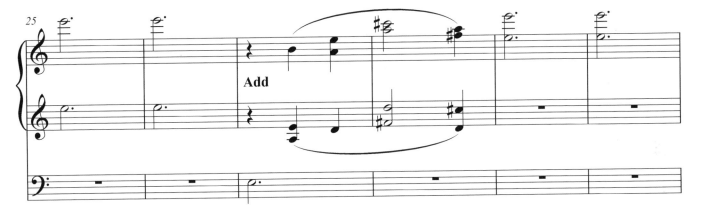

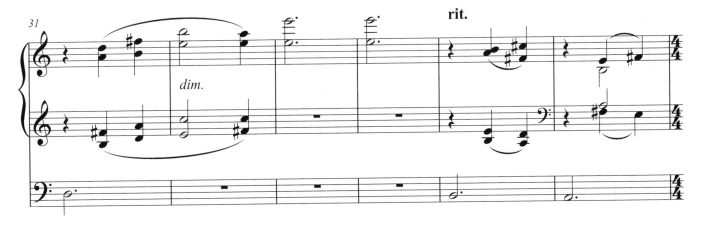

Danza ♩ = 92

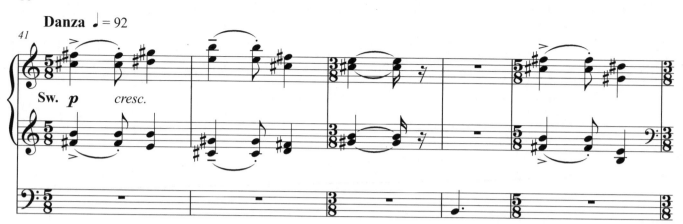